ONLY HERE
BECAUSE
HAVE NO
OTHER
OPTIONS

UPSET
ABOUT
YOUR
PROMOTION

ANOTHER
SH*T
DAY
HERE

NOT A
F*CKING
MONDAY
PERSON

INHALE
GOOD SH*T.
EXHALE
THE
BULLSH*T

TOO MUCH S*HIT, TOO LITTLE PAY

INHALE
GOOD SH*T.
EXHALE
THE
BULLSH*T

NOT GIVING
A F*CK
IS BETTER
THAN
REVENGE

CHEER
THE
F*CK UP

LET
THAT
SH*T GO

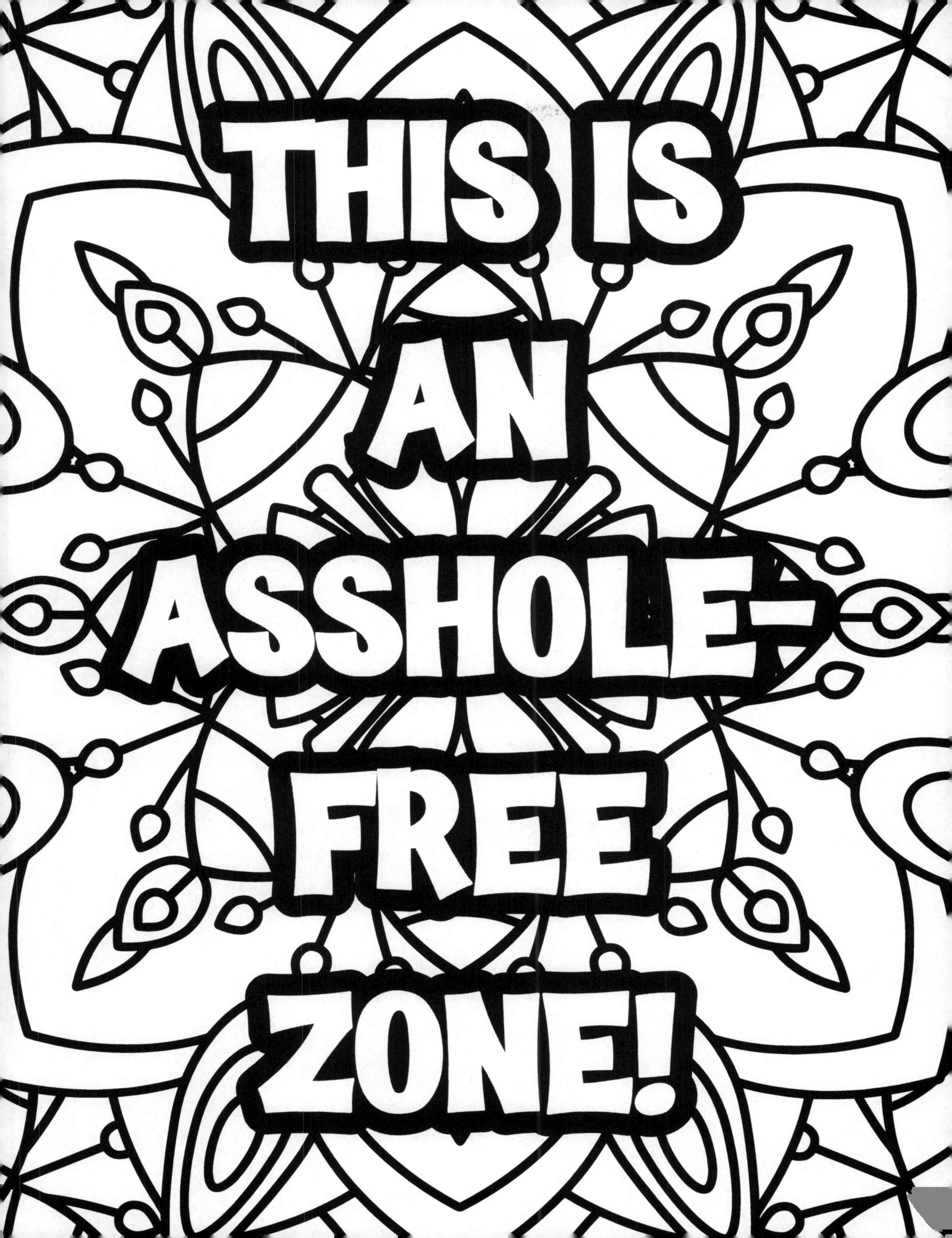
THIS IS
AN
ASSHOLE-
FREE
ZONE!

SCREW
THIS!
I'M GOING
HOME

FRIDAY
IS MY
SECOND
FAVORITE
F-WORD

NO, I CAN'T
WORK, THIS
WEEKEND
MOTHER-
F*CKER.

I'LL TRY BEING NICER IF YOU'LL TRY BEING SMARTER

HOW ABOUT
NEVER?
IS NEVER
F*CKING
GOOD
FOR YOU?

WHO THE
F*CK DIED
AND MADE
YOU
A BOSS?

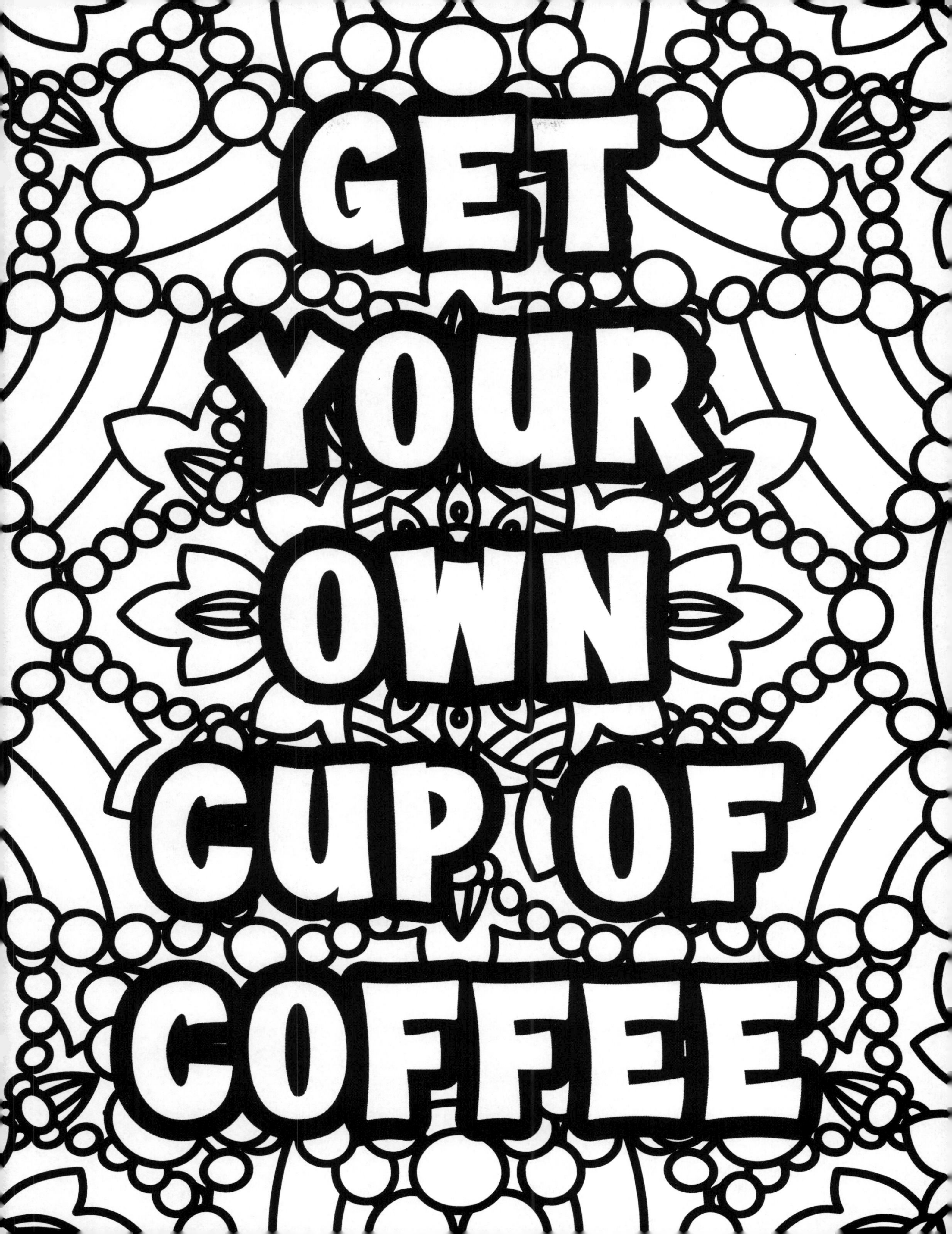
GET
YOUR
OWN
CUP OF
COFFEE

SORRY
I CAN'T
WORK
TODAY

SORRY
I CAN'T
COME
IN
TODAY

DON'T LIKE THE WAY YOU SPEAK TO ME

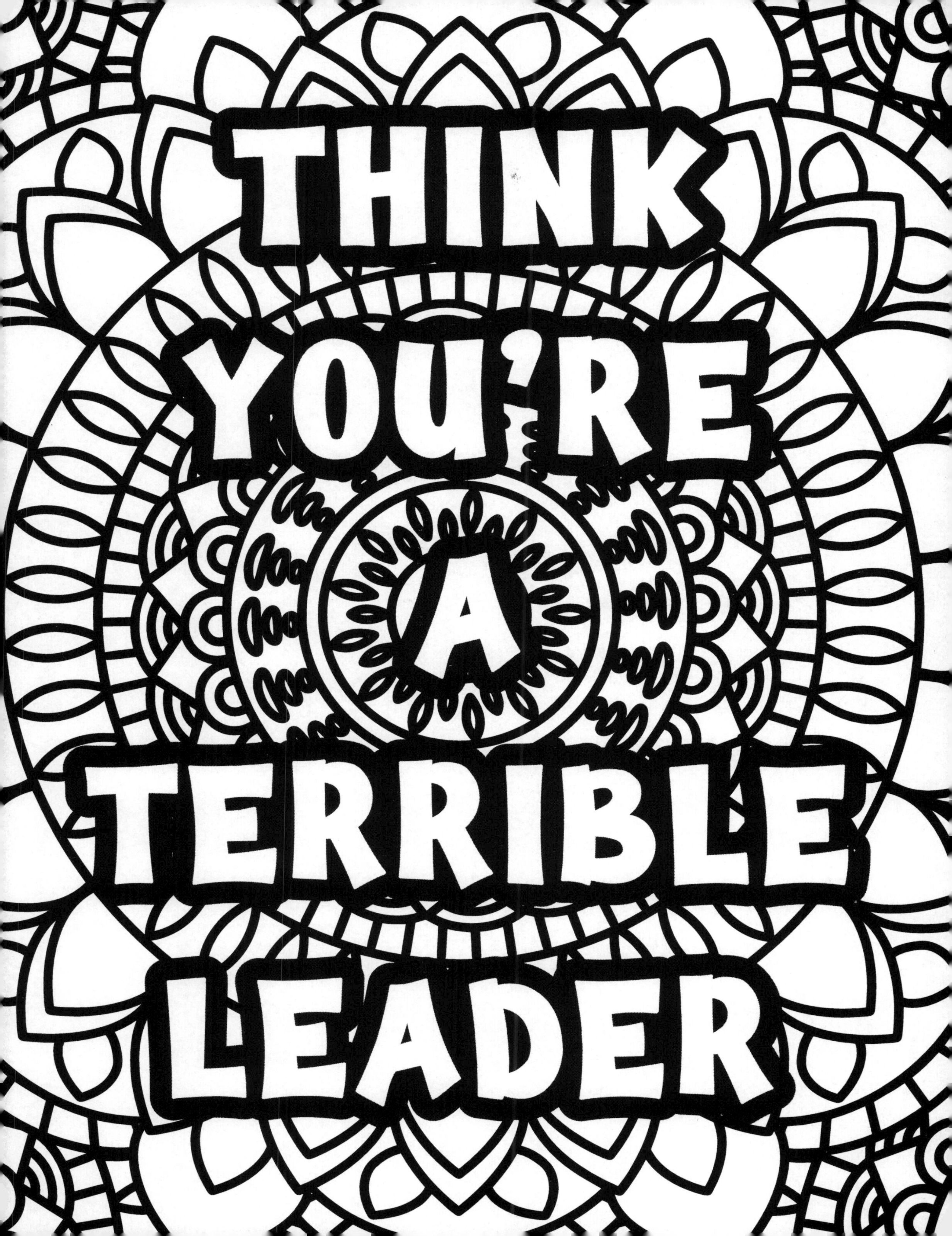
THINK
YOU'RE
A
TERRIBLE
LEADER

CAN'T
STAND
THE WAY
YOU
SMELL

THINK
YOUR
IDEAS
ARE
POOR

DON'T
THINK
YOU'RE
QUALIFIED

CAN'T
STAND
THE WAY
YOU
TALK
TO ME

WANT
TO QUIT
AND
NEVER
RETURN

DON'T
AGREE
WITH
COMPANY
POLICIES

THINK
THE
COMPANY
WILL
FAIL

HATE
THIS
JOB

I WISH
I COULD
IGNORE
YOU

ONLY HERE FOR THE MONEY

SECRETLY
LOOKING
FOR
ANOTHER
JOB

ONLY HERE FOR THE MONEY

CAN'T
STAND
WORKING
WITH
YOU

WHICH
D*CK
ATE
MY
LUNCH?

ZERO
F*CKS
GIVEN

YOU
F*CKING
ROCK

YOU
F*CKING
ROCK

EAT
SH*T
AND
DIE
AS*HOLE!

WHAT
THE
F*CK
IS THAT
SH*T?

I GAVE
ZERO
F*CKS
TODAY

DON'T
BE
A
D*CK

I'M LATE
F*CKING
DEAL
WITH
IT

CALM THE F*CK DOWN

HEY
F*CKFACE
DO
SOME
WORK!

I AM
NOT
DOING
THAT
SH*T

I DON'T
GET PAID
ENOUGH
FOR
THIS
SH*T

WE
OFFER
FREE
LESSONS
IN
CRAZY

MAY
CHOKE IN
ALL THE
SH*T
YOU TALK

Made in the USA
Las Vegas, NV
07 December 2023

82278865R00057